THE JOURNEY...

Continues

A new dance - a complete worshipful
experience

THE JOURNEY...
Continues
A new dance - a complete worshipful experience

C. Patrica Noble

THE JOURNEY...

Continues

A new dance - a complete worshipful
experience

C. Patrica Noble

A publication of The Publisher's Notebook Ltd

THE JOURNEY... CONTINUES
Copyright© 2014 Cynthia Patrica Noble

ISBN: 978-976-95940-9-8
Book cover design: The Publisher's Notebook Ltd
Front Cover Photography: Images used with permission from SmartShag Photography

Quotations and scriptures are taken from the New King James, New International and King James Version of the Bible.

Published by: The Publisher's Notebook Ltd

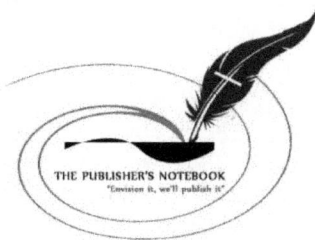

THE PUBLISHER'S NOTEBOOK
"Envision it, we'll publish it"

http://thepublishersnotebook.com
email: publisher@thepublishersnotebook.com
Telephone: (876) 782-1866

DEDICATION

I dedicate this book "The Journey...Continues," to all the founding members of Praise Academy of Dance for believing that God can make something beautiful out of nothing. Your commitment to the vision of the dance in worship, your faith to believe that God will complete what He started, your encouragement, love and prayers has spurred me on. I love you all.

Sam Green, Dadre Verley, Claudette Clarke, Homer and Angela Slack, Delone Flanigan, Dawn Walker, Tracy-Ann Williams, Sharon Samms-Bett, Sharon Gordon, Hope Wynter-Cooke, Horace Cooke, Fredrica Wright, Fredrica Stewart, Sandra Neil, Jennifer Murray and Paulette Lindsay. My prayer is that you will continue to trust the God who knows and sees the end from the beginning.

CONTENTS

FOREWORD - PASTOR DINO NICHOLAS

The Journey... **Continues"**, is aptly titled, as its author has been on a transformational journey for over twenty years. In this time we have witnessed the steady rise of the Ministry of Dance from a place of obscurity to now a place of prominence. It is now a true art form in the church and in the wider society. Thanks in great part to Cynthia Patricia Noble.

In her humility she would never accept such an honor, however her body of work speaks loudly to all that God has indeed called and anointed her to do in this generation.

As I read through the pages, I sense the love; devotion and passion of Aunty Pat towards her students and Ministry. You will be captivated by her simplicity, her realness and her submission to the spirit.

I fully endorse this book, not only for persons in the worship art of dance, but for all Christians who desire to have a deeper walk with God. Aunty Pat is an artist not only with bodily expression but gifted and anointed with the word of God to draw us into the secret chambers of the heart of our heavenly Father. This book is destined to become a classic.

Pastor Dino B. Nicholas
Founder -the Power House Ministries
Westmoreland, Jamaica

i

FOREWORD - KEISHA CAMPBELL

Have you....
- ❖ Lost your passion for dancing, and now you just dance out of routine?
- ❖ Been procrastinating in returning to the dance?
- ❖ Been longing to start dancing for the Lord?
- ❖ Been trying to understand what dancing for the Lord is all about?

If you have answered yes to any of the above questions, then this book is for you. Chapter after chapter, page after page pours forth with the passion and commitment Cynthia Pat Noble (Aunty Pat) possess for the Lord and for the dance. In this book she has engaged us on a journey to the new dance. Her approach to the book has lifted passion and commitment off the page right to where the reader is located and inspires you to move not just to dance, but, evokes a deeper yearning for intimacy with the Lord.

"It is a dance of restoration, reconciliation and transformation...." Aunty Pat.

"It is one which says God's love is unconditional, unfathomable, reaching those who are on the mountain and those who are low in the valley; a dance which speaks from the heart and comes with a piercing of the sword...." Aunty Pat.

Aunty Pat has had numerous fascinating, beautiful, miraculous experiences with the Lord through the dance and she has taken us on some of those journeys in her book. The ease at which she pulls you into the pages makes reading the book effortless and convenient.

You will want to make it apart of your devotions to help usher you the dancer into a more gratifying relationship with God. Aunty Pat offers insights that will transform your approach to dancing for the Lord. Take a rewarding, refreshing and passion evoking journey for the dance with Aunty Pat. As you read this book, enter the journey of a lifetime.

Keisha Campbell (past student)

FOREWORD - PASTOR HOWARD ROACH

Many books have been written about worship, with an emphasis on voice, drama, and instruments. Yet, not much is either seen or said about dance. Even in our Caribbean context; the use of our God-given, indigenous creative expression is often seen as "not of God" and therefore was strictly opposed in many traditional and non-traditional settings. For those and other reasons, literature pertaining to the use of reggae and or any dance associated with that genre, as a "legitimate" form of worship has been largely ignored...until now.

Who better to give voice and insight to these two incredible gifts of God, than Pat Noble, a humble servant of God, whose journey continues as one who is a trailblazer in the area of Christian dance ministry. Pat's passion for the lord and worship are easily captured in these pages. The journey continues is a personal examination, with a biblical foundation, giving each reader a gentle invitation, to renew their individual and corporate worship expression, by combining movements to the sound of gospel reggae. The writing in the book of Isaiah puts it this way *"let them give glory unto the Lord, and declare His praise in the islands". Isaiah 42:12.*

This book will inform, inspire and impact each reader, ministers (servants) and creative arts ministries. Transformation is a hallmark of this journey.

Howard Anthony Roach
Praise and Worship Leader

FOREWORD - DAVE & MARCIA WEEKES

God said to Pat Noble, "Who are you edifying when you are dancing like this?" Pat Noble went into a corner and said, 'God, anything you want me to do, I will do."

It's the scenario outlined above that qualifies this great woman of God to write this book. This mighty woman of God obeyed God and as a result was dancing in church long before dance was considered appropriate or even considered a real ministry. She has defied great personal odds and has pioneered a path in the area of dance ministry throughout the Caribbean and beyond.

I have known Pat Noble for nearly 20 years and I can attest that the message in this book is penned by a woman of God who has given her life sacrificially to serve the kingdom of God. She has completely answered the call of God to walk in her prophetic destiny as a powerful dance minister of God.

I sincerely believe, that through the Holy Spirit, ***The Journey...Continues*** will inspire readers to passionately pursue Him in complete obedience to God's Word. Pat Noble not only dreamed and talked about what she wanted to do for God she stepped out in faith and placed herself in a position to be used by God. As you read this book you will discover the life of a woman that has been totally surrendered and dedicated to obedience to God.

This book is a timely expression of the truth about loving God and desiring to do what He wants. Pat Noble has waked the walk of humility, servanthood and faithfulness and is indeed a fitting servant to share these truths with those who are desirous of serving God in the Arts.

The Journey...Continues will help any young minister answer the questions - "How do you know you are called to the ministry of dance?" How do I obey the call of God on my life? How do I maintain a life of holiness while serving in ministry? How do I stay faithful to the cause in the face of disappointments and adversity?

The Journey...Continues seek to enlist people everywhere to take the journey of obedience and sacrifice to God, will you take the journey today?
Dave & Marcia Weekes
Artistic & Managing Director
Praise Academy of Dance, Barbados

ACKNOWLEDGEMENTs

I acknowledge the Creator of all things—the Father, God the Son, God the Holy Spirit for granting me favour to proceed in writing this book. My appreciation goes to Marcia Weekes, Artistic Director of Praise Academy of Dance Barbados; Claire Green; Rev. Dr. Donald Stewart, Pastor of the Portmore Lane Covenant Community Church and Pastors Peter and Pat Morgan, founders of Covenant Community Church for believing in the vision. Appreciation also goes to my sisters Norma Blake, Monica Samms and Donna Samms-Reid; brother, Keith Samms; nieces, Sharon Bett, Maxine Williams, Andrea Hofatt, Staceyann Fletcher and Sacha Malcolm for standing in the gap for me.

To the teaching staff, ministry team, Board of Directors, intercessory team, students of Praise Academy of Dance, I appreciate you for weathering the storms with me. I extend appreciation to typists Simone Parker, Lajeane Cooke, Stacy-Ann Fletcher, Tasha Coombs and Candace Morgan for their voluntary effort.

Thanks to Pastor Dino Nicholas and sister Claudette Cooke who prophetically affirmed God's desire for this book to be written, so dancers and worshippers can release the sacrifice God requires from each of us for the redemption of the dance.

Thanks to Women of Virtue & Grace dance ministry of Portmore Lane Covenant Community Church for being women of strength, encouragement and enthusiasm. Your laughter, times of fellowship and your determination to be worshippers in the dance have deepened my love for Jesus, the Lord of the dance.

To my former church family—Portmore Lane Covenant Community Church, Portmore, I express great appreciation for your prayers and your undivided attention as a support group. Portmore Lane will be transformed because of your faithfulness to the vision.
A SPECIAL THANK YOU TO **LANA EVANS** for her assistance in preparing this book.

Thank You. You are all SPECIAL.

INTRODUCTION

"And whatsoever ye do, do it heartily as to the Lord and not unto men."
Colossian 3:23

Dance is movement and all movements originated at the beginning of creation, when the Holy Spirit moved upon the waters in Genesis 1:2. This scene had life, beauty, excitement and peace, making this art form special and unique to God.

It is unique because of its visibility, expressiveness and fluidity. This pure form of dance was given to the church but was usurped by the enemy who defiled its purity. Dance was then ostracised by the church. The world, on the other hand, adapted the dance to a culture that portrays sensuous movements and display of the body in a revealing state.

I was arrested by the Holy Spirit as one of God's servants to help to redeem the dance and return it to its original position, where God intended it to be. Redeeming a dance means redeeming a culture. This is the time that God is restoring all things for His Glory.

This book introduces the elements that God shared with me from His heart so that the dance should not be just a mere performance, but a dance of PURPOSE—transformation of body, soul and spirit.

The Journey...Continues relates to the above scripture and speaks of (4) four categories connected to the ministry of dance:
1. "Whatsoever ye do" - Offering
2. "Do it heartily" - Willingness
3. "As to the Lord" - God Pleasers
4. "Not unto men" - Men Pleasers

OFFERING

Offering deals with the surrendering of the heart, giving full commitment of self to the giver who gave us the gift. This gift is not for self-gain, but is to be imparted so that the Kingdom of God will be extended here on this earth. An offering requires careful thought because it is like making a vow to or covenant with the One who made the deposit in you.

WILLINGNESS

Willingness is letting go of selfish ambitions and worldly gains so that the delivery of the gift will bring lasting and impactful results. The gifts we received must be operated out of a vessel of a broken Spirit and a contrite heart, one that is willing to make sacrifices in order for people to be restored. Each time that we present this gift, it must be out of love and appreciation for the One who suffered the shame and disgrace on the cross for us—our Saviour Jesus Christ.

GOD PLEASERS

David, in Psalm 16:8a says, "I have set the Lord always before me." The presentation of the gift must not be taken lightly, as our objective at all times should be to give honour and praise to God for redeeming the gift of dance and restoring it to the church. Our focus should always be directed to God, because the dance is the easiest art form to be contaminated and distorted by the enemy. Let us therefore consistently allow the Holy Spirit to sanctify us in order for God's presence to totally immerse us.

MEN PLEASERS

Many times dancers do this activity out of a love for the art form instead of being called by God to appropriate the gift for the body of Christ. Our motive is what counts, so do not allow the enemy to warp what God created for His glory.

The mistake many of us make is to become personal with the gift, so our time is not spent becoming intimate with Jesus Christ but bringing attention to the 'I': "*I* began the ministry; *I* determine when, where, how and what to dance instead of being directed by God." John 12:43 says, "For they loved the praise of men more than the praise of God." Also, take a hint from Matthew 14:6-11, where Herodias' daughter danced with the wrong motive before Herod. This dance pleased Herod, so he could not refuse granting her wish in giving her the head of John the Baptist on a platter. Herodias' daughter's wish was granted and this was negative. Let us remember at all times that the dance should bring hope, peace, joy, healing, salvation and deliverance.

Romans 1:25 says, *"Who changeth the truth of God into a lie, and worshipped the creature more than the Creator, who is blessed forever, Amen." The gift must not be worshipped; it will become idolatrous in the sight of God and He is a jealous God. Our worship must be to the Giver, the Great God of All who in the beginning was God and is God.*

THE PREPARATION

Trust His Heart
Romans 12: 1-2 —"I beseech you therefore, brethren, by the mercies of God, that you present your bodies a living sacrifice, holy, acceptable to God, which is your reasonable service. And do not be conformed to this world, but be transformed by the renewing of your mind, that you may prove what is that good and acceptable and perfect will of God."

This scripture is the basis on which the mind starts its renewal process, where the mind is now experiencing changes in metamorphosis state. The mind is now being reshaped, remodelled and redirected by the word of God through His Holy Spirit.

Each dancer, having entered into this new relationship, will be encumbered by doubts and fears as to how his/her body will respond to this new change. Questions, questions coming from every angle: Can this change become real and will I ever be accepted in the Beloved to do the dance He requires of me?

Yes, I know it is possible for you because He did it for me. The dissection begins when He sees the desperation, the threshing floor posture and the heart of a deer panting for a stream to quench its thirst. He hears our throbbing hearts and runs to the rescue with an outstretched arm and a ready embrace.

This is a place of death to our feelings, emotions and desires. God Himself steps in with no condemnation but an unconditional love for one more worshipper/dancer to place a dent in the kingdom of darkness.

It is a new experience where The Father Himself redirects and orders our steps in the way He chooses. We have to be willing at this time to go through The Refiner's fire [1] so the purification process can begin.

The process is tedious, stressful, tearful and painful but memorable. During this time you begin to understand the love of God and reflect on the Garden of Eden experience where Adam and Eve had fellowship with God.

Here is where I learnt to trust His heart and realised how important dance is to His heart. He listens to our desperate cries of 'why not someone else.' But when His purpose is to be carried out He will chase you until you become pliable in His Hands for the redeeming of a culture created for His glory.

---

[1] Malachi 3:2-3

R - E - G - G - A - E

A NEW DANCE HAS EMERGED OUT OF DIFFERENT SITUATIONS AND EXPRESSIONS OF A PEOPLE

Many persons believe that dance is limited to a particular type of movement and style. God knew that other dimensions needed to be birthed so He allowed me to go through a period of waiting where He was able to take me on a journey where I would become teachable and open to receive this new dimension.

This new dimension motivated and challenged me not to be ashamed of my body, but to use it as a vehicle for the Word to be delivered in a transformative and radical way. Most of these dances use the feet to do movements which are directed to the destruction of the kingdom of darkness.

Owing to the new generation of young people that has emerged, the facets of dance have changed. So reggae, hip-hop, folk, jazz, street dance and stepping are now enabling them to minister in the way that is more comfortable to them. God is creative; therefore He not only wants us to redeem the dance but to perfect the gift He has deposited in us.

The training I received at Jamaica School of Dance, now Edna Manley College of the Visual & Performing Arts, was basically techniques, styles and movements developed by particular dancers which are used in choreography. My testimony in the dance is based on interpretive worship, where a divine impartation from God was released through the prophetic that brought a new focus to dance; that is, I received an Interpretive way to choreograph by the Holy Spirit, using words from a song, phrases and the scriptures to make movements, giving the movements meaning. Sometimes the different techniques I learnt are also used with an interpretation in choreography.

Based on the church culture in Jamaica when Praise Academy of Dance was birthed, 'reggae' was considered bad for the church –it was considered as the devil's music. The only idiom of dance that I could do was modern dance which has a ballet foundation and was the 'correct' type of dance. The idioms mentioned earlier were unacceptable as it relates to dance in the church. God wanted to redeem dance and He had the perfect plan for it. Owing to the fact that the Academy is one of the agents of change in Jamaica, our God saw the need for reggae and folk to be a part of the puzzle. For this new dance to be effective, this particular idiom of dance had to be redeemed and transformed. This type of dance is warfare and 2 Corinthians 10:4 states that "The weapons of our warfare are not carnal but mighty through God to the pulling down of strongholds." Thus our determination was to press through, trusting God to fight the battle for us to break this mindset. I have become a lover of acronyms so God gave me one for REGGAE:

R – Redeemed from the hands of the enemy
E – Energetic
G – God-given
G – Good
A – Anointed
E – Everlasting

Did you know God had a sense of humour? God used the very thing that the church had considered to be shameful to bring transformation. Reggae took on a new meaning for us in that ministry in the inner cities gave us the opportunity to be identified with the people.

- This is their heartbeat, enjoyment, laughter and nightcap. We now had a dance to destroy mindsets, transform lives and bring a more relevant and practical way to deliver the Word of God. Reggae carries a style that is unique in its form and delivery. Owing to the restoration of dance in the kingdom of God, reggae dance possesses certain outstanding effects upon people:
- It produces a decisive effort among the dancers to go in and possess the land that God has given us.
- It brings deliverance and total abandonment in Jesus Christ - whom the Son has set free, is free indeed [2] - and causes a release of the power that God has deposited in His people.
- It releases tension and gives flexibility.
- It diminishes inhibitions and fears.

---

[2] John 8:36

- It evokes a feeling of unity and a bond in the believers, because it is the voice and heart of the people.

Different parts of the body have different functions to play in this type of dance:

Hands – God gives us power in our hands to suppress the evil one
Action – to press, flick, tear-away, cut, chip; movements are usually sharp or sustained – Psalm 18:34

Feet – the feet symbolise dominion and authority.   Psalm 8:6 – God has placed all things under our feet.
Joshua 10:24 – 'Put their feet on their necks. This action exemplifies God's promises to make our enemies our footstool (Psalm 110:1).

Actions symbolise suppressing, stamping, stepping on and leaping over the enemy

Head – moves side to side, up and down, circle

Hips – are used to give accent

Shoulders – are used for isolation and carriage

Other parts of the body – are used for carriage and to help add dynamics

Other Effects:
- bringing change
- tearing down, treading down, trampling on
- hammering out without reservation
- enjoying what God has given us

- restoring what the enemy stole
- setting the foundation for the standard to be lifted

God continues to restore what originated in Him and He needs us, being kingdom people, to play a major role in the restoration process. Let us be ready to appropriate the gospel by saying, "Lord whatever you are doing in this time through the Interpretive Dance, don't do it without me."

DEVELOPING THE NEW DANCE

Committed To The Vine

For the new dance to be kept alive we must be connected to God as the VINE with us as the branches using these three words: Faith, Obedience and Love.

These three ingredients keep my relationship exciting with God:

Faith –"Without faith it is impossible to please God, because anyone who comes to Him must believe that he exists and that he rewards those who earnestly seek Him." (Hebrews 11:6)

Obedience — "Now by this we know that we know Him if we keep His commandments." (1 John 2:3)

Love –John 15:12 – "My command is this: Love each other as I have loved you."

1 Corinthians 13:13 – "Now abideth faith, hope, love but the greatest is love."

As I reflect on the initial move of God in my life – it was *faith* that took me on the journey with Him, with me not knowing the pitfalls I would encounter. The stages He took me through were like that of a child's development. In John 15:5, Jesus says:

"I am the vine, you are the branches. He who abides in Me, and I in him, bears much fruit; for without Me you can do nothing."

Abiding (living, settling in) is a tangible experience that produces worship and tears and

8

leads to faith—bringing the unknown to reality. The Vine, which is Jesus Christ, brings a vertical connection through which an intimate relationship is produced. This vertical connection has caused me to realise that as a branch I must be attached to Jesus Christ; if not, I am dysfunctional – suffering from malnutrition. Here is where the pruning process begins, which will show you how many pounds of flesh still exist. Jesus says, "No flesh can glory in my presence" 1 Corinthians 1:29.

The times of waiting at his feet were many often times unbearable, lonely and frustrating, but the results were awesome, inspiring and transforming. **Obedience** is key to our relationship with God. 1 Samuel 15:22 b states: "To obey is better than sacrifice and to hearken than the fat of rams." Saul's relationship with God was shattered and he was rejected as King over Israel because of his disobedience. Once God establishes a covenant relationship with you, you have to always remember the responsibility that is entrusted. It's not that I did not fail God many times, but once the Holy Spirit convicted me I tried not to justify my actions. Disobedience brings curses into our lives and the enemy uses this to abort visions and covenants.

Love is the governing principle that should control all of us as believers. When all prophecies and other gifts have faded away, love is the only ingredient that will bind and hold a relationship together [3] . As an academy of believers we still are trying to understand the

---

[3] 1 Corinthians 13:8

word **agapeo**. This is the unconditional love God has for us and if we do not love those who we see, then we can't say we love God. His instructions were clear to us to embrace other dance ministers/ministries to show love in a tangible way.

Through the pruning process of the vine, as a branch I am beginning to understand the real meaning of love.

LOVE - being ready to die for someone

putting the interests of others above mine

giving the last of what I have to someone

giving the best of what I have

devoting time and resources to change situations

not expecting anything in return

Note this, I am not saying this is where I am but this is where I want to be, and each dancer/believer should aim to reach this place in Christ. Reaching this place means complete trust and dependency on God, knowing that it is better for God to accept us in His Kingdom doing good works surrounded with love and compassion than for him to say, *"Depart from me*

I know you not[4]" when no one spoke like me in tongues or walked in the prophetic as I did. I am learning not to become empty as tinkling cymbals and a big sounding gong [5]. This unconditional love affords us free access into the throne room of God and the ability to have a conversation – where God speaks to us about how we should live and dance as believers. Therefore there has to be a throne room experience where there is no shifting of our focus as to place degrees on whom we should love or when we should love. Distractions will come but we must not allow them to block the sight of our vision and the reason why we can love without being partial.

When God births a vision in us – faith, obedience and love form the banner under which He wants us to dwell. Psalm 91:1 says "He that dwelleth in the secret place of the Most High shall abide under the shadow of the Almighty." There is a secret place in Him where He awaits us so that we can dance His heart. This secret place, places us in His security, therefore our abiding causes an aroma to trouble the nostrils of our Heavenly Father, so we cannot help but live a life of worship in and through dance. Abiding in His presence causes the angels to be alert and fight on our behalf – catch us before we fall, watch us when we sleep or when we dance or walk. Worship in the dance becomes more meaningful when the connection to the Vine remains constant because worship has to fulfil God's purpose. Psalm 149:6-9 outlines the authority the saints of God have when our

---

[4] Matthew 7:23
[5] 1Corinthians 13:1

relationship with Him becomes more intimate: *"Let the high praises of God be in their mouth, and a two edged sword in their hand, To execute judgment on nations, and punishment on the peoples, to bind their Kings with chains, and their nobles with fetters of iron; to execute on them the written judgment – this honour have all His saints."*

Question: Should worship be just a Sunday service prayer meeting, or devotions?

No, worship and abiding is day-to-day practical Christian living; it is a lifestyle. Any gift or talent that has been deposited in us has to have some form of origin, and that origin is God. Let us therefore go back to basics: Who created us? Who deposited the gifts, talents in us? Who should receive the glory?

Failing to abide creates abnormality in our impartation, witnessing and fruit bearing. As dancers/saints of God we have an authority that affords us access to the throne of God. Liberty is extended to us to abide in His presence, which allows us to be seated in heavenly places in Christ Jesus. This is a position of hope, trust and assurance. Why should we forfeit such a great privilege? As dancers our responsibility is an awesome one, because we have to give God a worship that pleases Him.

God is not interested in partial commitment, obedience and time but He desires our full attention. Dance is worship, so the attitude of our hearts becomes a posture of total submission. Therefore since His presence is a tangible experience let us always remember that if we are faithful in what we offer, God will reward our faithfulness.

There are some hindrances that always show up to distract our focus—fear, insecurity, prejudice, low self-esteem, compromise, unforgiveness, hatred and pride. But with this new and fresh move of God let us plant seeds of peace and love for the edification of His church through the birth of this new dance.

There is a new dance in every person who has been called into this new experience; however, you can only receive same when the relationship is cemented in purity and commitment. Hesitation and procrastination defeat the purpose, but a demonstration to declare and bring change causes God, Jesus Christ and The Holy Spirit to be always with us and working through us.

I can hear the cry of the children, as their tattered dusty feet and tear-stained faces yearn for something more to be imparted to them. They are the next generation who are dying without finding their purpose. Let us who have been sealed with His Spirit of the dance or any art form radically take ourselves behind the veil where God is waiting to supernaturally transform and bring to life this new dance. Be ready to raise your level of expectancy so that you can see new dances from His throne and from His heart.

If you believe that God has imparted such a talent in you and would love to get an idea of launching into the deep then you can try these elements which will produce a new level of excellence in all areas:

Awareness of the body.
- Choreographic skills, which will give the interpretive dance a stronger foundation
- Simple choreography to create a better and lasting impact
- Visible impact in the interpretive, which brings great conviction to the audience
- Communication and clarity, which evoke righteousness.

Will you be a part of this remnant? Seek to develop your technique and other skills of the art, deepen your knowledge of God through His word and encourage yourself in Him daily. Do not allow the negatives to wear you down, but build yourself up in activities that highlight Jesus Christ and the affirmation of His love.

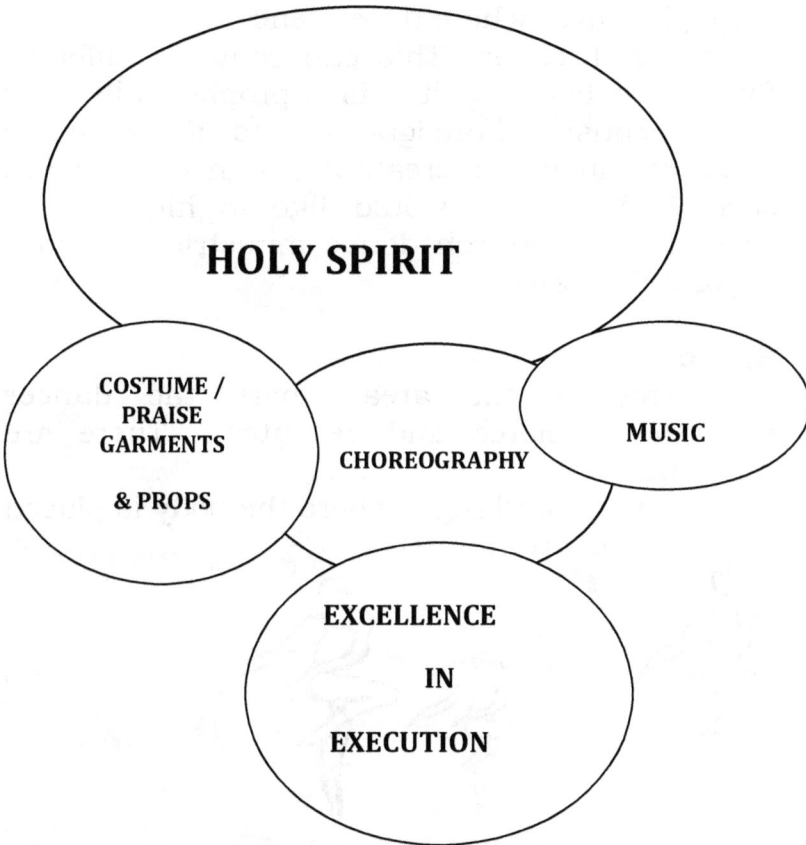

CHOREOGRAPHY

Choreography should be carefully explored through prayer where dependence is on the Holy Spirit for direction. This can come in different forms –whether it is prophetically or spontaneously choreographed to a particular piece of music. In creating a dance there are several elements I would like to highlight in order for our church dance ministries to move beyond the walls.

Space:

This is the area where the dancer performs; explores and executes. There are different levels:
low; medium; and high (where the body is placed in heightened positions)

All dancers do not need to remain at the same level throughout the dance - within this space the body can move using different shapes, pathways and formations.

Shapes:

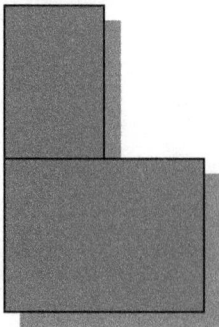

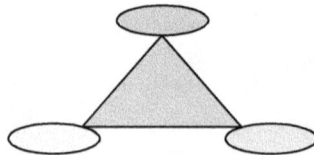

Curves:

16

Pathways- the route the dancer's body takes to travel through the area:

Lines:

Others:

T

X

Time:
Making use of the rhythm e.g. if the music is in 4/4 time the choreography does not have to be on that beat throughout.

Syncopation- accents
Speed: double or triple the speed, going against the normal rhythm.

Energy:
quality of the movement (sustained, percussive)

To create interest in the choreography, the following can be done:
- Change focus
- Add locomotor movements for transition
- Walk, skip, run, jump, leap, hop, glide
- Use non-locomotor movements-twist, stretch, bend
- Stillness (very effective)
- Sequences can be done in half time (twice as slow) or double time (twice as fast)

- Utilise the canon – which is movement done consecutively
- Repetition – recurring design
- repetition creates a picture in the mind of those viewing
- it sets the tone for the choreographer to vary the sequence
- Dynamics—change of direction, time, levels or energy

Consistently reading the Word is a plus for the choreographer because it gives you a new vocabulary of unique movements each time. As much as possible one must try to avoid using the same movements for every dance.

Movements can be varied in many different ways and this adds height and depth to your choreography, which holds the interest of your audience or congregation.

The choice of music is key to any choreography bearing in mind the following:

- the suitability for age group – adult or child
- Too many times the music we choose for our children is too advanced and unappealing. Music used should be enjoyable worshipful, happy and interesting.
- the words should be audible so that the audience can become a part of what is happening on stage. If it is instrumental then it should portray a particular theme.

COSTUME/PRAISE GARMENTS

Costume can either enhance your dance or detract from it. I find that the best thing to do is to pray for inspiration to create costumes/praise garment for a particular dance. Choices of colours and designs are very important aspects in costuming.

In Exodus chapters 28 and 39 the colours which are outlined for making the priestly garments are blue, purple, scarlet and gold. These colours are significant for ministry because of the divine stamp that was placed upon them at the construction of the tabernacle.

COLOURS SPIRITUAL SIGNIFICANCE

blue	victory, peace, Holy Spirit
purple	royalty, worship
scarlet (red)	warfare, blood of Jesus
gold	heavenly, worship, praise

OTHER COLOURS (NOT IN THE TABERNACLE)

white	purity, righteousness
green	growth, prosperity (life eternal)
black	depression, bondage
yellow (gold)	joy, exuberance, glory
brown	earth
silver	redemption

Another dimension that brings excellence to choreography is props. Props are objects that can be utilised in a dance effectively, for example chairs, stools, balls benches etc. along with banners, flags, ribbons and strips of cloth.

As the people of God called forth to be choreographers, let us remember that as priests, we are expected to present excellence in our dance. All the elements mentioned before have been placed in our hands by our Heavenly Father. Mediocrity is not of God, so as His called out ones (the ecclesia) we should be determined to acquire the skills that are needed to develop this art form.

HEALING & DELIVERANCE
THROUGH DANCE

Pure Vessels Filled With The Holy Spirit

Question: What is Healing?

Marpe is the Hebrew word for healing. It means restoration of health; remedy, cure, medicine and tranquility.

The Hebrew word for 'deliverance' comes from the verb **rapha** – to heal. Salvation is God's rescue of the entire person; healing is His complete repair of that person.

In Greek, **paradidomi** means 'delivered.'

From my experience, healing and deliverance will only occur when there is a pure vessel filled with the Holy Spirit, a vessel abiding and embedded in the Word, a vessel that carries the manifested presence of God. Dance is therapeutic: it relaxes the mind, brings peace, joy, restoration and healing that no other art form possesses. Thus transference of spirits is something that cannot be ignored. The ministering vessel should therefore be constantly and consistently living according to the principles of God's word, i.e. to be holy as God is holy. It is therefore imperative that our relationship with God be in constant renewal every second, every hour, every minute and every day. For this vessel to remain pure, one has to live an honest and pleasing life that is obvious even to the natural man.

The life we live has to be laid on the brazen altar so that the flesh can take no glory. A vessel of purity places a heavy demand on the individual, but if we know the purpose into which God has called us, then the task will become easier. Healing through the dance has to come with a price of digging deep, staying connected to the source - which is God - and allowing the Holy Spirit to do the impartation.

Dance plays an integral part in worship and because many pastors and leaders have still not come into that understanding, we the forerunners cannot allow the enemy to stifle the vision God has for the dance. God's commission in Matthew 10:1 says "And when he had called His twelve disciples to Him, He gave them power over unclean spirits, to cast them out and to heal all kinds of sickness and all kind of diseases." God placed an authority in us, along with different gifts and talents, when we received salvation. The word is preached in different forms, therefore it should be active, direct and uncompromising so that the signs will follow. The dance, which is a practical demonstration of the word, should come with this kind of impact, counteracting, diffusing and upsetting the enemy's domain.

Through telephone calls, media reviews, dialogues and friendly discussions, many people stated that they have been affected positively by:

The power and anointing the movements carry
The interpretive experience : many times, when people view these dances they are either

23

delivered from a situation, healed, feel convicted or become transformed

If God's tangible manifested presence is not there, then the dance is ineffective. In Luke 4:18 Jesus quotes from the book of Isaiah 61:2 when he says "The Spirit of the Lord God is upon me, because he has anointed me to preach the gospel to the poor, he has sent me to heal the broken hearted, to proclaim liberty to the captives and recovery of sight to the blind. To set at liberty those who are oppressed; to proclaim the acceptable year of the Lord." This then should be our main focus. Jesus' ministry was based on results. Whatever ministry we are involved in should enhance worship, and lives must be impacted, challenged and changed.

Remember, the carrier of God's anointing is a threat to the enemy, so we have to make sure that the vessel reflects the characteristics of Jesus Christ—holiness, purity, righteousness and the fruit of the Spirit[6]. Since we know that ministry is a privilege that comes with a responsibility, the Spirit of humility must be birthed in us individually and collectively.

Looking at twenty-one years of ministry we can truly say that through our mistakes, failures and weaknesses which are our testing grounds, God has been with us. Our ministry times have had different shades; each one is never the same. This has taught us to see how much our dependence is upon the Holy Spirit. Through our ministry, many have received salvation, deliverance and healing. Many of our dancers

---

[6] Galatians 5:22-23

now in the academy came because their lives were impacted. An interesting factor about the dance is that the life of the dancers has been and continues to be transformed through different aspects, bringing transparency to their lives and the ministry.

They are learning how to practically live a lifestyle of worship and how to deal with negative vibes which try to penetrate them from different angles. The dancers have come through, and continue to go through different experiences, which have enabled them to know and practise a lifestyle of worship, because what you take in is what you give out.

MAINTAINING THE TEMPLE

Spiritual, Physical & Technical Maintenance

Temple – The Hebrew word **heychal** means tabernacle or sanctuary and refers to the inside of the temple. 2 Chronicles 29:16 says, "Then the priests went into the **inner part** of the house of the Lord to **cleanse** it and brought out all the debris that they found in the temple of the Lord to the **court of the house of the Lord**. And the Levites took it out and carried it to the Brook Kidron."

Maintaining the Temple for worship in the dance falls in three categories:
Spiritually – **inner part**
Physically – **cleanse / Brook Kidron /outer part**
Technically – **debris; fine-tuning**

Spiritual Maintenance – Hebrew **hagladzo** means sanctified, dedicated, consecrated, separated; a state of holiness.

This begins with sanctification, a setting apart. Rom. 12:1 says, "I beseech you therefore brethren by the mercies of God that you present your body a living sacrifice, holy and acceptable unto God which is your reasonable service." Sanctification is an ongoing process which one has to really want to go through in order for service to be effective. This can be compared with the processing of gold before real gold can be seen. Malachi 3:2-3, says "But who can endure the day of His coming? And who can stand when He appears? For He is like a refiner's fire and like a launderer's soap; He will sit as a refiner and purifier of silver; He will purify the sons of Levi, and purge them as gold and silver that they may offer to the Lord an offering in righteousness."

For our worship in the dance to be pure, Christ has to be the purifier and refiner in our lives, so that we can be clean to offer service and worship that is acceptable unto God. We cannot afford to offer the Lord less than our best, anything less is unworthy of His Holy name. Proverbs 3:5-6 says, "Trust in the Lord with all thine heart and lean not to thine own understanding. But in all thy ways acknowledge Him and He shall direct thy path." This process forces us to rely on God our Father, who will give us spiritual wisdom, in order that we can reject the wisdom of the world. God's wisdom should be our focus; it propels our energies and lifestyle so that whatever we do with our temples will bring honour and glory to Him. Galatians 5:16 says, "I say then; walk in the Spirit and you shall not fulfill the lust of the flesh." There is a constant conflict between the Spirit and the flesh; therefore we have to continually submit ourselves to the Holy Spirit who will enable us to become victors instead of victims. This requires us to practise His presence which causes us to develop a life of holiness.

Holiness– **hagosune**[7] in Greek (Hebrews 12:10) – means 'the quality or a condition of holy disposition in purity.' Holiness separates the believer from the world and consecrates us to

---

[7] Greek translations are from the Spirit Filled King James Bible (Word Wealth)

God's service both in body and soul. It brings about fulfillment in moral dedication and a life committed to purity. Holiness causes every component of our character to stand before God for His inspection and meet His approval.

Holiness is not a possession, it is a position. It is something we are, not what we do. Both holiness and to be sanctified are from the same Greek root word **hagios**. Since our bodies are His temple, if worship in the dance is operated out of vessels that are not holy or sanctified, then worship is in vain. Let us therefore work out our salvation with fear and trembling[8], making a conscious decision to be holy, because God is holy.

There have been too many inconsistencies in our Christian walk. God is waiting for a remnant of imperfect people who hunger to be a sanctified people whom He can trust to carry His anointing to show forth His glorious praise in this earth that the unsaved and wicked will run to Him. The dancer who has been called by God has to rely totally on the Holy Spirit to be able to carry this responsibility.

Let us lay ourselves at the brazen altar and allow God to purge us that each time we dance unto Him an aroma will touch His nostrils and His presence will break the stony hearts, making acceptance of salvation easier.

Physical Maintenance of the Temple
In Hebrew the word **taher** means 'cleanse/cleansed', 'to make clean', 'to purify',

---

8 Philippians 2:12b

and 'to be pure, uncontaminated', 'cleansing physically, ceremonially and morally'. This refers to pure gold. Physical maintenance of the Temple can be related to the care of the place of worship – and we are the sanctuaries. Wherever one worships is considered the sanctuary. God requires a level of sacredness as we enter into His presence. God gives us different plans and ways to furnish His sanctuary and in the same way He instructs us about the care of our temples for service.

My relationship with the Lord had boulders, then rocks. Pebbles are still there, but through intimacy with Him I am beginning to understand the importance of physical awareness as it relates to His body being the temple. Careful recognition should be taken, because many dancers do not realise that our lifestyle and eating habits contribute to the physical maintenance of our temples.

Balanced Diet
Just as the inner man depends on the Holy Spirit and the Word for spiritual food, the physical body needs a balanced diet to remain physically strong. Within a balanced diet there is protein, carbohydrates, vitamins and iron. These nutrients not only contribute to growth and strengthening but protection against diseases and infections. If the physical part of our temple is maintained as God intended it to be, then we will not be faced with expensive prescriptions and will not depend on a particular medication to exist, but on Jesus Christ who is the great physician.

Eating a balanced diet gives longevity, healthy skin, ability to have abundant life and to attain the highest achievements in life. 3 John 1:2 says, "Beloved I wish above all things that thou mayest prosper and be in good health even as thy soul prospereth." God wants us to be healthy and so He has given us His word to guide our eating habits.

Exercise

Exercise is another requirement for proper maintenance of the temple. It develops alertness and awareness of the physical look of the body. It provides the body with relaxation and proper function of the organs. It reduces stress, strengthens the muscles, improves the intake of oxygen, helps the body to rid itself of impurities, improves circulation and increases our vitality.

Fellowship

A good relationship with families, friends and believers is another contributing factor to a healthy lifestyle. An environment with people who think positively develops unity, peace, love, concern and fellowship which set the foundation for trust and a sense of belonging.

Relationships on a horizontal plane enable us to have a vertical relationship with Jesus Christ. If we can recall, the life of the first church grew because of the joy in the fellowship (koinonia in Greek) of the believers (Acts 2:42).

In koinonia the individual shares an intimate bond of fellowship with the rest of the Christian society. Koinonia cements believers to the Lord Jesus and to each other. As relationships build, one has the tendency to become more involved in the activities of his/her ministry, church or any social pastime. One of the key elements for the development of any dance ministry is relationship.

This kind of atmosphere makes it easier for the Holy Spirit to release choreography, costuming, structure and unity.

Acronyms are one of my favorite ways in making illustrations real. Here is how I see relationships:

R – Realising that no man stands alone; one needs others to survive. Two are better than one – Ecclesiastes 4:9

E – Examples of our calling by Christ Jesus; following His steps – 1 Peter 2:21

L – Leaning on Jesus not on our own understanding; allowing God to lead us – Proverbs 3:5

A – Abandonment – abandoning ourselves in Jesus Christ like David and giving Him total control over our whole being – 2 Samuel 6:14

T – Thanksgiving, for the shed blood of Jesus Christ that has redeemed us so that we can be delivered from the kingdom of darkness into His marvellous light – 1 Peter 2:9

I – Inheritance; in Jesus Christ we have a rich heritage, which gives us security – because he chose us in Him before the foundation of the world. This inheritance gives us an acceptance in the family of God – Ephesians 1:4a, 11a

O – Order; everything we do in our different ministries, lifestyle, and response to each other must be done in order, so that God gets the glory – 1 Corinthians 14:40

N – Newness; the Holy Spirit (**pneuma** in Greek) has drawn us to Christ, convicts us of sin and enables us to live the victorious life, hence a newness of the inner man – Romans 8:2; 1 John 1:9

S – Serve; we have been called to serve each other in love, putting someone's interest above ours, giving of our best possessions to someone in need, serving with sincerity of heart – Colossians 3:12-14

H – Humour; humour in relationships is the breeding ground for honesty and ridding ourselves of inhibitions. –Proverbs 15:13

I – Increase; as we aspire in our relationships, we must remember that all we can acquire and our accomplishments come from God. – John 3:30

P – Place; our existence on earth must be purposeful and impactful. Therefore, once we are able to relate amicably on a horizontal plane with each other, we are confident that God has a place for us in His kingdom. – John 14: 3

Technical Maintenance of the Temple

Exodus 31:6b: "And I have put wisdom in the hearts of all gifted artisans that they may make all I have commanded them to do." God is a God of excellence, so when He calls us he places His Spirit in us who sharpens the skills to accomplish the labour with accuracy.

In my first experience, God's instruction to me concerning my previous training was to put the technique received behind me for a time, which He reactivated. God wanted the glory for the transformation, therefore, he initiated "Interpretive Worship" which is the dance we do. Then He began training us technically, allowing us to see that all creativity comes from Him. Within this technical training, He provided the different teachers with different abilities, skilled in their art to give their impartation. You see, it is the whole body that is involved in worship, so He makes my feet like the feet of the deer and he teaches my hands to make war – Psalm 18:33 – which is a combination of spiritual warfare and intercession. In our technical development we aspire for excellence in our stretches, leg lifts, elevations and synchronisation. When we are able to execute our movements well, we find that it is not about how far the leg can go, but when the leg lifts or the hand rises, what the unsaved or the onlooker receives.

Also, when the choreography is completed we want to know that the Holy Spirit will take the technique we have received to another dimension, because our dependence is not only on our technical abilities. Technical maintenance of the Temple helps us to concentrate more on becoming who God wants us to be and what He wants us to do with our training. As he trains us, He sends us out as His disciples to train others, so that His earthly kingdom can increase.

Technical maintenance also develops the correct posture and alignment of the body. We have seen where students, through this particular training, learn how to sit properly in a chair anywhere they are, or just maintain the proper carriage of the body.

As dancers there are many of us who have experienced injuries because there was no prior warm up. One's body does not get warm in one hour, so students are advised to begin this preparation before class. Injury prevention is emphasised because God desires that the whole body, His temple, be in service to Him.
Cooling down the temple is another aspect of technical maintenance which allows us to stretch our muscles, meditate on the goodness of the Lord for His continuous blessing and thank Him for redeeming the dance.

Remember, God created us in His own image, therefore he knows our technical abilities and the extent to which each of us can go. So let us give Him dominance over our temples so that they will always be fit and ready for service.

TEMPLE EVANGELISM

1 Samuel 2:18 – "But Samuel ministered before the Lord, even as a child wearing a linen ephod." Samuel made himself available to God for service at an early age. His lifestyle was exceptional, because he was in a place of submission. Samuel represents a prophetic dancer who is prepared to dance at anytime, anywhere, once the Holy Spirit gives the direction.

Why Temple Evangelism?

The Temple speaks of the body, how, when or what we use it for. The Hebrew word **heychal** means 'temple' or 'sanctuary.' Evangelism is telling others about the good news of Jesus Christ and the importance of living our lives to please God.

Temple evangelism is witnessing, using the body to carry out God's purpose. This witnessing begins in you, then spreads to the home, community and nation. Therefore, the life we live is the same at the base and away from base. Samuel's obedience caused him to avail himself to God and this produced a relationship of complete surrender and trust in God. He placed himself in a position where God became his central focus.

Once you are able to identify with Jesus Christ, He speeds up the evangelism process. Evangelism was not easy for Samuel right in the house of Eli but God intervened on his behalf, making the task easier. First came the intervention of God's presence, then the confirmation from Eli that Samuel was really hearing the voice of God. Samuel still experienced the spirit of fear, which is negative and had to be broken, so that the atmosphere in Eli's house could be changed. As a minister in the dance I too experienced that fear and I am sure many visionaries have gone through that negativity. When I allowed myself to be consumed with the Samuel anointing, temple evangelism was effectively transmitted.

Eli's relationship with God was severed; judgment and death were the result of complete disobedience. Since God cannot look at sin, he needs a prophet to deliver His word when he begins talking to us prophetically. This is where temple evangelism begins with a prophetic dance; reminding us that sin breeds death and destruction. Living a pleasing life of peace and fulfilment occurs when we know we are hooked up to Jesus Christ who is our umbilical cord. Have you resigned yourself to the place of submission and obedience? If so, God will use you. Temple Evangelism is sacrifice: David in 2 Samuel 24:24b says, *"Nor will I offer burnt offerings to the Lord my God with that which costs me nothing."* Ministry requires the act of sacrifice – giving ourselves to God, without holding back. Many times I had to sacrifice my time, energy and finances so that His ministry could go forth. What are you holding back that brings hindrance to your breakthrough? Many of us are not willing to walk in obedience and so we lose fellowship with God like Eli, where the gift is abused and our focus is shifted, leaving no room for the Glory of God to be manifested.

Once the glory departs, you are operating out of self.

The earth is crying out for the temple evangelists like Samuel who will seek the lost at any cost, who will speak a word in season and out of season, and who are not afraid of any face or system. God is waiting with outstretched hands, for those who are willing to die in order to live. *"For me to live is Christ and to die is gain."* –Philippians 1:21.

True ministry is serving Christ with all that He has blessed us with. "Aren't you tired of stagnation in your life, home, community, church and nation? Is there a throbbing in your heart and bubbling in your belly?" Dancers, worshippers, leaders and believers, let us be in hot pursuit of what God desires to do in the dance through temple evangelism. Let's not be left behind, but with forward strides be determined to reach those who are unreachable and bring life to the depressed, oppressed and those who feel like giving up. God has placed upon us His seal of authority.

Won't you pray this prayer with me?

Lord I realise that I have not treated your temple as a dwelling place for your Holy Spirit. Forgive me Lord for leaning on my own understanding, thus allowing the dance to be fruitless. I ask you dear Lord to rid me of all selfish ambitions, renew my mind, give me a heart like yours that I will only do what you desire to be done. I am ready to die so that you can live in me. My desire is to give you a sacrifice that costs me something. So Lord, take the dance, let it always be consecrated

37

to you. I surrender my creative abilities and my accomplishments. Take me Lord through the eye of the needle so that I can worship you freely. Amen.

TESTIMONIAL REFLECTIONS

Negative Experiences, Positive Experiences, Miracles & Wonders

"And they overcame him by the blood of the lamb and by the word of their testimony and they did not love their lives to death." –Revelation 12:11

Reminiscing on my life as a vessel chosen for the master's use I realised that the enemy wanted to destroy both my life and the vision of the dance in worship. When you are called by God and pursuing your purpose, the opposing forces are positioning themselves to abort, slaughter, distract and hinder. God's divine will must be accomplished, so whatever happens along the way of pursuit has to be in the plan of God.

If you find yourself in the vacuum right now experiencing spiritual drought as you try to understand your purpose in God, do not give up. This is the time when God desires your attention so that your dependency is totally on Him. Dancers and worshippers, you are special to God and because His purpose was established in you before the foundations of the world, you do not have to do this alone.

Below are various episodes which took place—direct attacks prior to ministry with positive endings, positive experiences, miracles and wonders:

1) Dog at Bay 1995

Place: 97 Old Hope Road

In preparation for Because of Him, our dance production in November 1995, I left the shelter of the tent where we met for classes and rehearsal, trudging gingerly across the playfield to the 'white house' where the bathroom was located. On reaching the dryer patch of the playfield the guard dog let himself loose. Parked nearby was an open-back van into which everyone scaled. I was transfixed and there were screams all around me when I felt the tail of the dog brush my thigh. I quietly said, "Lord cover me with your blood." Everyone was amazed; how did I escape such an onslaught?

It was the grace of God.

2) Ailments in my body 1996-2002

Abscess on my foot, cramps in my knees, muscle spasms in my right hand and colon cancer: through these experiences I am learning to really trust and depend on God even more. I discovered how real God is and that His promises will always come true. My faith continues to soar as I believe that "My God is able to do exceedingly abundantly above everything I can ask or imagine" –Ephesians 3:20. I experienced God's hand of healing, security, peace and comfort as He plucked me from the claws of the enemy.

Through these trials and this testing, I am able to be more compassionate and tolerant with different people who are sick. This has developed a warfare spirit within me, which makes me understand more about the enemy and his devious methods of distraction.

If you are sick while reading this book, claim your healing "In the Name of Jesus."

3) Fainting Dilemma
"When the enemy comes in, like a flood God lifts up a standard against him" –Isaiah 59:19. After conducting rehearsal for a performance, we were reflecting on the evening's success when out of the blue I fainted and ended up at the University Hospital of the West Indies. I was told that everyone had become frantic and confused as they accompanied me to the hospital. The doctor's examination proved negative for any medical condition.
JESUS CHRIST IS LORD OF MY LIFE.

4) Bahamas Experience 2000 - The Green Suitcase
On my arrival in the Bahamas as a facilitator for a Dance Conference, I discovered that one of my black suitcases was missing and I reported same to the authorities. The day of the conference dawned with excitement as we prepared for the opening ceremony. A phone call I received clouded this excitement: it was the C.I.D- Criminal Investigation Department - informing me about a green suitcase tagged with my name, containing 59 pounds of marijuana.

Shock and fear engulfed me. I was dumbstruck for some seconds and in a loud voice shouted that the green suitcase did not belong to me.

Two detectives, male and female, visited me at the hotel, and asked that I accompany them to the police station. The convener of the conference, Dr. Ann Peterson, advised an intercessor to go with me. As we entered the police station I was handed a document typed in fine print, requesting my signature.

As the paper entered my hand, the voice of the Lord cautioned me with these words, "If you sign the document you are signing your death warrant." Boldness overtook me and my reply was firm: I remarked, "What am I signing—signing to say the green suitcase is mine." I refused to sign it in the Name of Jesus. Immediately following that dialogue, another police entered the office with such pomp asking, "Who arrested her?" With the Queen's English I let them know my place of birth and that my Christian principles would not allow me to jeopardise my Christianity for few pounds of marijuana. Following that saga I was escorted to another area in the station, where the Lord explicitly told me to worship Him, making references to the three Hebrew boys, Daniel in the lion's den, Paul and Silas in jail. With scalding tears streaming down my face I became clamorously foolish in worship.

Instructed by the Lord to open my eyes, I gazed across the room as a policeman ambled towards me with a broad grin on his face and repeated the same words the Lord said to me. He took the bible and read Psalm 63 of which I will quote specific verses:

Verse 1—"*O God thou art my God, early will I seek Thee, my soul thirsteth for Thee, my flesh*

longeth for Thee in a dry and thirsty land where no water is."
Verse 2—*"To see Thy power and Thy glory so as I have seen Thee in the sanctuary."*
Verse 3—*"Thy loving kindness is better than life, my lips shall praise Thee."*
Verse 4—*"Thus will I bless Thee, while I live, I will lift my hands in Thy name."*

Closing the Bible he informed me that he was the boss's driver who should have left at an earlier time. His words to me were, "Had you signed that paper you would be confirming that the green suitcase was yours." With a voice of praise and thanksgiving to God, tasting my salty tears I worshipped with an explosion, just lifting up the King of Kings and Lord of Lords.

Where there is purpose that God wants to bring to fruition the enemy tries to wane your faith in God, but God always steps in on time, because the vision has to be accomplished.

"You Lord give perfect peace to those who keep their purpose firm and keep their trust in You"—*Isaiah 26:3.*

5) 1995-Production entitled *Because of Him* (Healing and Deliverance Through Dance)

A young woman was invited to attend our concert, owing to the death of her father, which had left her feeling depressed and confused. The song and dance, "Friend of a Wounded Heart", depicted a dramatic scene of a woman on drugs, who received healing. Several months after the young woman related her testimony about her healing and became a member of Praise Academy of Dance.

6) 1996 - At this production entitled *I Give My Best*, the main theme throughout was "Where will you be when the Lord returns?" Salvation came to many, mindsets were broken, a broken marriage was restored; others ran with haste from the Ward Theatre, not sure of their salvation. Those who had a relationship with the Lord were strengthened and motivated to diligently and consistently abide in His presence.

7) 1997-The South African Explosion

In July 1997, 28 members of Praise Academy of Dance attended the International Christian Dance Conference in Pretoria, South Africa, seven years after apartheid was lifted. Our Jamaican presence enabled us entry into a community that the Africans were afraid to visit.

As we blasted the sound system with songs like 'Mi Ting Pon Me' and 'We Have Message Fi Spread Abroad', the people left their selling and shopping just to see what we offered. They formed long queues just for us to touch and pray for them. This was tearful and rewarding.

For the first time, reggae took on a new dimension out of the Caribbean: mindsets were changed and racial barriers were diminished at the conference. What Gods originates He anoints and as Jamaicans we were readily accepted, because we did not suffer from racial discrimination. There was openness as we shared and talked to the people.

That earned us a bonus, because we were one of two groups who were asked to do a lunch hour concert, which was very transformational.

To God be the Glory.

8) 1997-1999 Cincinnati, Ohio- USA

1997- I was asked to be a dance facilitator at a Dance Conference, hosted by Dr. Lyrica Smith, to teach two workshops using reggae. After a time of meeting and sharing at the opening of the conference, she informed me that the Lord wanted me to teach the reggae to 300 people at the conference. I never questioned the Lord, I just said, "Daddy it's all yours—instruct me, lead me and I will follow." The music was "Mi Ting Pon Me" by Lester Lewis.

An electrifying warm up session, along with a sequence, was appreciated and the exuberance and energy were overwhelming.

a) The progression took a different form because the Lord requested me to use groups of seven across the floor, telling them that their starting position was Egypt and their finishing position was Canaan. On reaching Canaan they were to claim their healing, ask for salvation and deliverance.

At the end of the class all persons were lying prostrate crying in different tones. I was standing alone for ten minutes, after which all persons started hugging and crying on each other's shoulders. I was then informed that racial prejudice was a barrier in the churches and this experience through the dance had brought black and white together for the first time. I just said, "Lord thank you for obedience and learning to walk in your footprints."

God is to be praised.

b) Astonishingly a woman who attended the conference one week after major surgery to the back of the neck was wondering why she came. What blew our mind was that the dressing dropped off; she was healed, leaving no scar.

What a God!

c) In the conference, there was a white woman from London who did not participate in the workshop, because she felt it was 'too black.' After leaving the conference, she telephoned the convenor of the conference to let her know, she was rebuked by the Lord for her remark about the reggae and she was on her face before the Lord asking for mercy. She related that God told her that I was handpicked by Him, to help in delivering His people from racial discrimination using this type of dance.

There is no God like Jehovah.

9) 1999-- This was a repeat of 1997 where the yokes of racial discrimination and denominational barriers were crushed to the ground. Attendees shared with us about the freedom they experienced as they hugged and interacted with others.

His Name is to be praised.

10) 1998 --Barbados
Praise Academy of Dance was invited along with Papa San to "Taking it to the Streets", a ministry hosted by Dave and Marcia Weekes.

Reggae was done in a warfare mood and a supernatural anointing of the Holy Spirit was released upon Barbados.

11) 1999--We revisited Barbados

During this time the witches and warlocks trampled a certain section of downtown Bridgetown, leaving the evidence of corn grain behind. With the tools of Praise and Worship, the Blood and the Name of Jesus, a level of warfare broke out, bringing people out of their comfort zone, and taking them to a new level in the dance.

Without God it is impossible to complete any task.

12) 1998- Our first mission trip to England

Not knowing the whereabouts of any accommodation, a group of 31 dancers, wardrobe mistress, spiritual co-ordinator and cooks embarked on a journey. The folks in England called us crazy, but we knew we had to be there.

We encountered a group of people who cared and provided for us, which was so commendable, and we had to pinch ourselves, because it was not our doing.

We had an experience at a church call "Ruach", where we were to minister on the Sunday evening and hold a concert on the Thursday. However, the pastor was not enthused about the concert, so he advised us to do three dances. At the beginning of the second dance, he changed his mind and requested the concert.

The seating capacity was 2500, and on the Thursday not even standing space was available.

He alone is worthy to be praised.

13) 1998 –Production entitled 'The Church' At Stephanie Hall, Kingston, Jamaica

The Senior Department was getting ready to do a dress rehearsal for the above production, when God interrupted our devotions with this question: How can you present 'The Church' when there is so much unforgiveness, malice, resentment and lack of respect for leadership in your midst?

Following a time of confession, repentance, forgiveness and recommitment of our love for God and others, God's presence became so tangible that we had to wash each other's feet and cried tears of joy.

Out of this the production was a deliverance service, because demons manifested and healing came to a young woman whose name was Christine Haber. Since her deliverance all her household has been saved. God deserves all honour and praise.

14) 2000 Pretoria South Africa--Dunamis Christian Fellowship

In the year 2000 I was asked to conduct a reggae workshop. On my arrival I learnt they were a white church but they were then evangelising black people, which was a welcome sight, do not get me wrong; I am not knocking white people. On the opening night I danced to Chevelle Franklin's song "Radio Is Playing" and as the music pumped through the church all stood to their feet. Black and white joined in swaying and jumping to the rhythm. I had to dance twice.

This brought a new dimension to reggae. Thirty gospel CD's were sold off in two nights of the conference.

Majestic is He, who is, who was and is to come.

15) 2000-- Return Trip from South Africa

On my return trip from South Africa, the Lord instructed me not to eat the food that was being served. I thought the words were my own thoughts. So I proceeded, consuming all that was given to me.

Arriving in London, I felt really sick, and ordered some black coffee from Burger King. Nausea hit me and, crying out for God, I asked Him to forgive me for not obeying His voice. I arrived at the counter to be checked in and the Immigration officer requested my passport, which I found very strange, seeing that no one else had been asked. Having received my passport I noticed that my seat number was changed, but the seat number was not very visible.

Murmuring about the change I started to search for my seat only to see that my seat was upgraded to first class. Why? The Lord knew that I would be sick. Diarrhoea and vomiting engulfed me; I went back and forth visiting the place of "Letting Out." The flight attendants became concerned, placed me in the kitchenette and offered me some ginger ale. They escorted me to my seat where I slept until I reached the Norman Manley Airport. Even when we do not heed His voice, He still takes us through.

He is the same, Yesterday, Today and forever.

16) 2002--England

The ministry was impactful, infusing a reggae vibes appetite, which left many receiving salvation and deliverance, breaking mindsets and opening more doors for the gospel to be presented through dance. We visited Birmingham, London and Crystal Palace.

17) 2002--Infirmity of cancer

I was diagnosed with colon cancer in November 2002, which frightened me and all I could do was broadcast it locally and internationally, speaking to the demonic realms in the atmosphere that Jesus Christ is Lord over my life. The church prayed. I did the operation. I am healed, praise God; what the enemy meant for evil God turned around for His good.
"The enemy comes to steal, kill and destroy but God comes to give life and give it more abundantly" (John 10:10).

18) 2003--Gospel Fest Barbados

Marcia Weekes invited me to choreograph three dances for Gospelfest, an annual music festival in Barbados. The dancers were from several churches. A bond developed, which caused the dancers to share, interact and train together, not wishing to be anywhere else.

In 2003 Xtreme Impact- a Youth Conference was held in Jamaica, encouraging Christian youths to have an impact on each other. This brought the group from Barbados and they were automatically named Praise Academy of Dance, Barbados. Praise Academy of Dance Barbados was officially launched in December 2004. **Look at the blessings of the Lord.**

He who has begun a good work in us will complete it till the day of Jesus" (Philippians 1:6).

19) 2004-- England

We revisited England, extending our ministry to Cornwall. We reunited with the folks from other churches where we had ministered and participated in different concerts. Marcus Garvey Day, which was a secular event, gave us an opportunity to demonstrate the gospel using the medium of reggae. There was a great response.

From 1993 up to now, this new dance which was birthed in the heart of God as an expression of worship has left an imprint on the hearts of many people. Our ministry can only continue its journey of excellence through the reading and study and application of the word, prayer and fasting.

20) The Greater Allen M.E Dance Conferences, New York

2000, 2004, 2006, 2008

We owe gratitude to Minister Kathleen Turner and Pastors Floyd and Elaine Flake for sponsoring dancers and myself to participate in these conferences over the years. Sharing reggae in this forum offers a new scope for youths and young adults to minister on the street and inner city communities in total abandonment to Jesus Christ.

From our interactions with conference attendees, we found that reggae brings a freedom of expression which allows them to know that they can use the whole body to worship God in the dance.

At the Worship in the Word Conference Marvin Winans, after watching the Jamaicans dance, had to change his original message to "The Despised Dancer," using 2 Samuel 6:14, where David was despised by his wife Michal because he danced in abandonment to his God. 'Holy Ghost Church,' sung by D.J. Nicholas, was performed and ministered by the dancers with reckless abandonment in Jesus Christ. This was an electrifying moment.

Always give your best to the Lord.

21) Concerts and Ministries 1993-2013

The staff, Board of Directors and dancers have arrived at the conclusion that Praise Academy of Dance was orchestrated by God and belongs to God.

Each of us, through various experiences, can testify of trials we have been through before and after a ministry event or concert. We have experienced physical death of family members, car accidents, sicknesses, disagreements, theft of music and tape recorders for the concert and other distractions.

Through all of these experiences the scripture God gave us was **Romans 8:37-39**: *"Nay, in all these things we are more than conquerors through Him that loved us. For I am persuaded that neither death, nor life, nor angels, nor principalities, nor powers, nor things to come, nor height, nor depth, nor any other creature, shall be able to separate us from the love of God, which is in Christ Jesus our Lord."*
Although many times our flesh would get in the way, God always reminds us that He is always with us, no, matter how dim the situation looks.

The victories have been exhilarating; we thank God for His continued strength and love. All dance ministries, dance directors and dancers, I adjure you to seek God's face with diligence. Never compromise your faith. Always try to remain humble and let excellence be in your earthen vessels.

DANCERS' REVIEWS

Approaching the wide entrance of the gateway, on our way to another dance session, we had a clear view of the yellow and white tent. We were ready to experience rhythmic movements and hear sounds of different genres of music, but first, gather for class devotions at either end of the tent which was held by strong vertical metal poles drilled in a smooth concrete surface.

The tent became alive with blended voices during devotions to set our hearts, minds and bodies in the right frame to usher us into a productive class. African classes were interesting –the beating of the drum brought life to us dancers as we experienced some African heritage as our mouths even became active with sounds expressing appreciation and jubilation. There were times with the absence of 'bars' for stretching, the great poles were used to assist in what we called 'six o'clock'—one leg planted on the ground touching the pole and the other extended in the air.

The tent accommodated picture taking for concert magazines, laughter, tears, re-energized and refreshed minds and bodies. The yellow and white covering held vast memories and was the beginning of a great, hopeful and successful journey with God through dance.

Anicka Newsome

I can still remember the days walking into 97 Old Hope Road, where the first thing that greeted you was this huge yellow and white tent. Music was always floating through the air, whether via the cassette (yes, the cassette because CDs were not that popular at the time) playing in the stereo, the conga drum being played by Ms. Samms or of course Auntie Pat giving counts for a routine but instead of talking it, she had a rhythm and so she was really singing it. Now for those of us who had class next, if Auntie Pat saw us, we were usually told to go change (for those who were not in their dancing attire as yet) and go ahead and start devotions until she came to us.

Having devotions before classes and rehearsals remains vital to Praise Academy, because Christ is our foundation and if he had not intervened into Auntie Pat's life and given her this vision then there would not have been Praise Academy. The Lord has used Auntie Pat as a witness and a minister of the dance and many have come to know Christ through the various concerts and outreach programmes that have been held by Praise Academy of Dance.

I have learned a lot just being at Praise Academy and many can attest to that, but there is something that always stands out in my mind. Auntie Pat always reminds us that whether it is a regular class, rehearsals or an actual ministry event, we should always dance with excellence while giving honour, glory and worship to God. You can always hear Auntie Pat saying "Guys, don't wait until you get on the stage to start ministering, but let it start in rehearsals." Practising this has allowed several mini-worship sessions to happen during classes. I remember one night, at the same place, 97 Old Hope Road, there was a rehearsal for an upcoming senior concert and during the warm-up, Michael .W. Smith's song "Let it rain, let it rain, open the flood gates of Heaven" was playing and the night basically turned into a worship and deliverance session; and this was all because persons had begun the ministering before the actual concert. Therefore I hold that advice close to heart and continue to practise ministering during rehearsals. These are my few words, as I'm sure others have a lot more experiences to share.

Authurine Newsome

In 1994 I was one of four members of my church dance group. Back then we did not know much about liturgical dance but we were so excited to learn. After a year of existence, our little group was beginning to get exposure and we were invited to minister at a concert. As a result, we were told we would get some help to prepare for this concert—professional help. So in came this professional dance teacher who, in spite of our lack of dance training, was quite patient. She took our dance from 'square one' to something we did not even imagine possible. She took the simple steps we were doing and made them look exquisite, all the while emphasising the importance of execution. At the end of it all she told us about Praise Academy of Dance and that we should come join. All four of us started at Praise Academy of Dance, but as the months and years went by, I remained.

So began my more than 15-year relationship with Auntie Pat and Praise Academy of Dance; one I have never regretted.

Being a part of Praise Academy of Dance has not only built up my dance technique and exposed me to international training and experience through workshops and travel, but most importantly edified me on my spiritual journey. The concerts, retreats, ministry team and devotions have all played a unique role in my overall spiritual development and have provided much needed support over the years. One of the significant things Auntie Pat used to say to me in my early years at Praise Academy of Dance was, "Annelise, God has put so much inside you."

At the time I had no clue what she was talking about (I couldn't see it in myself) but I accepted this encouragement to press deeper into God. Simply put, being a part of Praise Academy of Dance has been one of the best parts of my life and I am truly grateful to God for putting me in it.

Annelise Christie

Praise Academy of Dance is a place of very fond memories. First thought ... Aunty Pat, an admirable and genuine soul who loves The Lord with all her heart. Called and blessed of God with divine talent, she is also generous and willing to share her knowledge and experience with others. She is happy to see others grow in Christ and encourages the development of identified talent in others. She also stands guard in prayer where she sees any of her now numerous children deviating from or walking in righteousness.

Aunty Pat and I met years prior when we were both students in different programmes at the School of Dance, Kingston, Jamaica. We were again reunited through a mutual friend and a lasting friendship began. The years that followed at Praise have been some of my most memorable. Aunty Pat and I grew in respect and love for each other as we gradually worked very closely together. She was a constant source of encouragement especially when I was venturing into novel territory.

The impact of Praise Academy in my life is more internal than external and continues to unfold in my growth with The Lord. Relationship is undoubtedly the biggest gain in my life—first, with God, then with others. In addition to my foundation at church, this was an environment of spiritual nurture. I also developed what I hope to be some lasting relationships with members of the Praise Academy family who hold a special place in My heart.

This is an environment where I found genuine care and love expressed in its various forms. I was encouraged and supported through some difficult seasons of life and perhaps if it were not for the creative and expressive outlet at Praise Academy, life could have taken a different course.

My most treasured lesson at Praise Academy is the transition from secular dance to worship of the Living God. The daily routine of a half hour devotional time prior to class is so firmly rooted in my psyche that other formats prove lacking to my spirit. This time set a positive tone for what was to follow.

I arrived at Praise Academy at a time when a spiritual renewal was in motion. There was an increased focus in the dancers, an awareness of greater dimensions in worship and a more committed approach to the development of their talents. I saw full committal of energy and time during class. The final product was always beyond what I had expected as it tapped into the divine and rendered results in the audience that only God could do.

I also observed a difference in the spirit of the dance. Secular dance excludes God, no matter the embellishments. It was here that I recognised in a more concrete way that one's spirit needs to be trained in its relationship with the Giver and engaged along with the soul and body in dance. With our spirits available to God, He is able to work in and through us and do a far greater work in our audiences than merely entertain and amaze.

Audiences and dancers alike experienced deliverance from demonic oppression; a number entered into a personal relationship with The Lord; some convicted of sin; others comforted, encouraged or strengthened in their spiritual walk or simply entered into a time of worship.

Dance took on new meaning as it was used as a means to an end and not the end itself. Here, one's entire being was able to fully engage the Ultimate Presence. He alone is able to accurately measure the quality of our offering and is able to free us from all encumbrances.

I also learned the importance of spiritual preparation. Though this ought to be a way of life, we learned as we grew together. There was always some spiritual stocktaking to be done prior to every production. It served as way of clearing any hindrances between us and The Lord as a result of problems in our relationship with one another or breaches in our union directly with Him.

I learned that when entering or dwelling in God's presence individually or corporately, cleansing from all sin is a must in order for our offering to come before Him as a sweet-smelling savour. As night follows day, once this happened, there was a divine liberty that accompanies The Holy Spirit.

On occasion, differences were worked through during or after the production, hence continuing to work character in all who were willing to see the matter through to the end. Through it all, Aunty Pat withstood many varying opinions, clarified issues and stood in defence of those who needed it. Though at times it was a heavy load, she demonstrated the command to " ... always pray and never give up" and was a constant example of forgiveness.

Praise Academy was also a place where I had the opportunity to discover and develop some talents. My first publicly viewed choreography outside of Praise Academy was a huge flop! I painfully learned that a dancer does not necessarily make a choreographer. Aunty

Pat later encouraged my first choreography at Praise, which she closely supervised while artfully and patiently guiding its evolution.

Through this, I learned hands-on principles of choreography that was more interpretative than abstract in form (more meaningful for most audiences) and contrary to what I had experienced in secular dance.

Though I have only scratched the surface of choreography, I owe a huge debt of gratitude to Aunty Pat. Since then I dabbled in other aspects of theatre production as a result of her kind encouragement. As we worked closely together in my latter years at Praise, this allowed me to observe the depth of her dependence on The Lord and serves as an example of faith and prayerful perseverance in action.

I desire to see Praise Academy grow into a place where each individual, being well trained in God's Word, lives a life of complete surrender as a result of cultivating an intimate relationship with Him; a place where He is truly The Lord of the dance; where bodies are offered as living sacrifices to Him allowing His will to be done and His kingdom to enlarge in the earth.

Andrea Plunkett

DANCE COMMENTARIES

These dance directors are considered as pioneers in Christian dance and are still pursuing excellence in this art form. These quotes are either from them personally or from literature written by them.[9]

COMMENTARIES BASED ON THE WORD, 2006

***Kathleen Turner* – Director, The Allen Liturgical Dance Ministry**

As directors and choreographers we must use the gift of liturgical dance that we have received to serve others, faithfully administering God's grace in its various forms.

God's grace can only be administered faithfully if God's Holy Spirit is influencing us. Each dance we choreograph must have thought, scripture, intention, charge and discernment behind it, so God not only gets the glory, but God speaks through what we have been charged to do.

***Reverend Eyesha K. Marble* –Assistant Director—Allen Liturgical Dance Ministry; Founding Director – National Liturgical Dance Ministry**.

It was at that time in history; God spoke greatness into every organ of your body, to accomplish a mighty work in His Name, and to give Him all the glory.

---

[9] Greater Allen Cathedral Worship in the Arts conference booklet, 2006

He called you to draw people unto him, to witness with integrity to the unsaved, to be the salt of the earth and the light of the world. (Matthew 5:13)

He called you to set a standard, to be a person of good influence for the world. You cannot walk loosely like the world. You are to change the status quo. You are called to be a change agent who allows God to order your steps in His word.

Pamela Hardy — Co-ordinator of the National Baptist Congress; Founder of 'Gathering of the Eagles Training Institute'; National Network Co-ordinator for Christian dance Fellowship, U.S.A.

Dancers it's time for the new release of God's anointing. For those who are hidden in Him it's time for new dances, His dances. God is changing things in His house, making us for His purposes. New winds are blowing in God's kingdom.

BELIEVE IT, RECEIVE IT; IT'S OUR TIME-- STAY FOCUSED.

MINISTRY IMPACT

Ephesians 3:20 – "Now unto Him who is able to do exceedingly, abundantly above all that we ask or think, according to the power works in us..."

What is Ministry?

The Hebrew word for 'minister' –**sharat**– in Hebrew means 'to wait on, to serve, to attend' and refers to the tasks which the closest servants of God or the King are assigned. (1 Chronicles 15:12) The priest and Levites in their ministry in the tabernacle served God. Examples of significant positions of service include Joseph to Potipher, (Genesis 39:4) Joshua to Moses (Exodus 33:11) and Elisha to Elijah (1Kings 19:21.) The scriptural use of the term conveys yieldedness, servanthood and obedience.

Ministry should therefore operate out of a yielded vessel where the one ministering has a definite call, a call of servanthood and obedience. Many of us who are worshippers, preachers, dancers, actors and actresses need to take an inventory of our individual lives to find out if the words mentioned above are evident and visible in our ministry. A call to ministry should not be of operating out of the mere fact that 'before I was saved I was a dancer or an actress.' This call should be divinely orchestrated, so that the receiver's life will be transformed.

Ministry involves the whole person, and because we are called to be Levitical worshippers, our lifestyle has to be in accordance with the principles of God's Word.

Can we truthfully say that as ministers we have been effective witnesses in our ministry? Do we have evidence of people's lives been changed or healed? If not, our labour in the vineyard is in vain. Let us not fool ourselves; every wasted moment is the clock ticking away in eternity, because one life that should have been changed was hampered by the kind of ministry you or I delivered.

Impact

Impact speaks of visibility; a picturesque, lasting impression. Impact can be negative or positive. Negative impact in dance breathes transference of spirits- frustration, carnality, stagnation and wrong conceptualisation of dance in the kingdom. This kind of impact forces the onlooker to want to compare the secular with the spiritual. People will therefore be drawn to watch more secular performances because the flair of movements and costumes mean more to the flesh. Hence we are defeating the purpose of the arts. Positive impact arouses interest, thus fulfilling the great commission of evangelism.

Ministry impact is a visible picture of the anointing which creates an atmosphere of positive vibes, bringing light, life and establishing a lasting effect on the mind. When we reflect on the life of Jesus Christ, the greatest of all champions - Conquering Lion of the tribe of Judah [10] - we see positive impact which eradicated demonic forces, brought dead to life,

---

[10] Revelations 5:5

made blind to see, opened deaf ears, restructured lame feet and made stony hearts become hearts of flesh. His ministry impact was not faked neither was it compromising. Jesus set the example for us, so as His offspring, what we deliver should be of the same effect or more. Jesus, in John 14:12, says, "Most assuredly, I say to you, he who believes in Me, the works that I do he will do also; and greater works than these he will do, because I go to My Father." Jesus has faith in us; we need to reciprocate this faithfulness so that more people's lives can be affected by our ministry.

Ephesians 3:20 that was mentioned at the beginning of this chapter contains the imagery of dependence, trust and confidence in a God who surpasses all understanding. It is always so refreshing to know that once you allow God to use the little you have, preparation becomes easier and the results are overwhelming.

Over these twenty-three years of focusing on the purpose God has established for my life in this nation I have arrived at one conclusion in Jeremiah 29:11 – "For I know the plans I have for you, says the Lord, thoughts of peace and not of evil, to give you a hope and a future." God has my life in His hands, because so many times I felt like giving up, but just that still small voice reminded me that he had conceived me in His mind first, before conception in my mother's womb.

More and more we are learning to have an ultimate focus on Jesus Christ, the One in whom we live and have our being[11]. For each ministry engagement done, the impact has been varied because each environment calls for sharp discernment on how to pray and intercede to recognise the strongholds or demonic spirits. In some areas we experienced the operation of territorial spirits and various strongholds, so alertness and wisdom had to be operative. The spiritual battle increases, but with intercession the breakthroughs are tremendous.

For any ministry to survive, consistency, continuity, humility, accountability and transparency have to be the foundation principles, because they show that the ministry has its origins in God. Never start a ministry unless it is what God desires.

Having travelled to several countries, namely the United States of America, Australia, South Africa, Canada, England, Barbados, Puerto Rico, Curacao and Trinidad, we have come to appreciate and love our Father God for birthing in us the Spirit of the dance. The same Holy Spirit that raised Jesus from the dead is the same Holy Spirit who resides and ignites us to be world changers.

Through our ministry we have developed and established meaningful relationships locally and internationally. Owing to the impact of our ministry these relationships are serving as referrals for us, in that our invitations extend far and wide. Many local and international dance ministries contact us for consultation in the areas of biblical foundations of dance, technical

---

[11] Acts 17:28

training, costuming, reggae technique, use of props and choreography. We are honoured today to be such a vehicle of inspiration, motivation and development. Our desire is to continue to be the example-setter for excellence and professionalism in worship in the dance.

Everything is dependent upon the heart. Why do I want to be a worshipper in the dance? Motive is the key for lasting effect and transformation. We extol and adore our risen Lord and Saviour Jesus Christ for affording us to come this far by faith. It is our determination to allow the Holy Spirit, the "allos"[12] to dwell and operate through us so that we can do exploits for Him.

The book of Acts reveals the transfer of Christ's authority and mission to His disciples to go and preach the gospel to the entire world (Matthew 28:18-20, Acts1:8.) It is the creative power of the Holy Spirit that convinced them to go, act, establish and expand. The same Holy Spirit is at work in us today, to do the same. True ministry has been demonstrated to us by the disciples and the apostles in the early church and should be characteristic of any dance ministry.

We at Praise Academy of Dance are learning to apply the words and phrases below to our lives and the ministry so that we will always remember that the impact a ministry brings has its roots embedded in the Holy Spirit.

---

[12] **allos paracletos (Greek)**—'another of the same kind'; i.e. , Jesus left and sent another in His place –John 14:16

- **Boldness:** Acts 4:31   Hebrew—***parrhesia*** (outspokenness, unreserved freedom, freedom of speech.) Here it denotes a divine enablement that comes to ordinary and unprofessional people exhibiting spiritual power and authority.
- **Power: *dunamis*** Acts 4:33 Dunamis means energy, power, might, great force, great ability, strength. The dunamis in Jesus resulted in dramatic transformations.
- **Doubting nothing:** Acts 11:12 ***diakrino*** connotes a conflict with oneself, in the sense of hesitating, having misgivings, doubting, being divided in decision making, or wavering between hope and fear.
- **Wisdom:** Acts 6:10 ***sophia***—practical wisdom prudence, skill, comprehensive insight, Christian enlightenment, correct application of knowledge, insight into the true nature of things.
- **Teachable spirit:** being able to be taught by anyone; the humbling of oneself
- Suffer: ***pascho*** Acts 17:3 –to experience ill-treatment, roughness, violence, or outrage, to endure suffering, and to undergo evils from without.
- **Fervent: *zeo*-**Acts 18-25 – living fervour, fiery hot, full of burning zeal.
- Humility: Acts 20:19
- ***tapeionophrosune***—modesty, lowliness, humility, a sense of moral insignificance and a humble attitude of unselfish concern for the welfare of others. It is a total absence of arrogance, conceit and haughtiness.

- **Give:** Acts 20:35 *didomic*—granting, allowing, bestowing, imparting, permitting, placing, offering, presenting, yielding and praying. The giver takes on the character of Christ, whose nature is to give.
- **Zealous**: Acts 22:3 *zelotes*—burning with zeal, having warmth and feeling for or against; deep commitment and eager devotion to something or someone, imitator. Paul rejected his previous zeal that caused him to become a persecutor of the church but rejoiced in his **zelotes** for the Lord Jesus Christ.

Our objective is to continue to be an effective ministry with consistency as we allow ourselves to be always led by the Holy Spirit.

THE CHALLENGE: *WHO WILL GO?*

The John the Baptist Anointing is referred to in Matthew 11:12: "And from the days of John the Baptist until now, the Kingdom of Heaven suffereth violence and the violent take it by force."

This verse suggests
Imprisonment
Speaking Life to Dead Situations
Getting out from behind the walls
Doing the John the Baptist dance, i.e. dance without fear on the streets, in the prisons, at the sea-side, in the schools, in the homes of the unfortunate

John the Baptist was imprisoned because of his conviction to deliver the message of salvation to those who were lost and in despair. The anointing imparted to him was a radical one, which placed him in danger so many times. But his responsibility was one of faith in God to destroy hypocrisy and self-centredness through the power of Jesus Christ.

If your objective is a radical one then you will be willing to be imprisoned, tortured and killed, all for the glory of God. Do not think I am harsh, because the life of John the Baptist was spent in the wilderness. Wilderness can mean dryness, inactivity, hopelessness and suffering, yet he went through all of this in the same way that Jesus Christ went through suffering.

Are you still dancing behind the walls? Who do you really dance for? Is it for the same righteous folks who want to see a new costume or a pretty dance? Dancers, it's time to be radical for Jesus Christ. People are dying all around us, the sick are increasing in numbers and the prisons are overflowing. Who will go? Who will dance with spontaneity and power? The dance is preaching the Word with abandonment, without fear or prejudice. If God has called you for a time like this in His kingdom, then you will say like Esther, "If I perish, I perish."[13]

What is the purpose of the dance? Is it only for worship on a Sunday or Saturday, a harvest festival or another festive occasion or is it to build up the saints and to help to destroy the kingdom of darkness? Our nations are crying out for HELP!! This is an individual and a collective mandate that God has place on our lives. We have allowed ourselves to become F-A-T in so many conferences. Where is the evangelistic approach that God gave us in the Great Commission in *Matthew 28:19-20*? *"Go therefore and make disciples of all the nations, baptizing them in the name of the Father and of the Son and of the Holy Spirit, teaching them to observe all things that I have commanded you; and lo, I am with you always, even to the end of the age."*

Evangelising the streets and communities should be the challenge for all dancers and worshippers. God desires each community to be a haven of rest, a place to fellowship, and a

---

[13] Esther 4:14-16

place of personal liberation as the citizens unite, sharing their unique gifts and talents. Today our nation is being destroyed by negative forces. We need a remnant of people with the John the Baptist anointing to expose the kingdom of darkness.

If God is sending us, He will protect us, but He allows something to happen only for His glory. We are the light of the world; however, those who are in the dark continue to live in the dark because we have hidden ourselves behind walls. Walls of hypocrisy, fear, prejudice and lack of compassion have crippled us and we have become alienated from the world, building a wall of partition.

How then can we effectively bring change to our lost communities and nations?

If we reflect on the impenetrable cities of Jericho and Ai[14] we will remember the spiritual authority that was displayed. It was the exercising of their faith coupled with obedience that caused them to be victors and not victims. Spirits of hopelessness, despair, depression, rejection, lust, prostitution, drugs, child-abuse, demonic depression and rape stem from the destruction of families. These are strongholds that the enemy has used to keep our nations in bondage. We as dancers have been given this authority to bring hope to the nations. Ezra 7:28: "So I was encouraged as the hand of the Lord my God was upon me; and I gathered chief men of Israel to go up with me." This authority comes with knowing our true identity in Christ.

---

14 Joshua 6:8

72

Radical anointing brings radical change – (Proverbs 29:18) : "Where there is no vision the people perish." It is imperative at this time that we try to create and implement strategies using this John the Baptist Anointing:

- ❖ **Street Dancing- do the dance of the people interpretively on the streets**
- ❖ **Invade the school curriculum with this new dance**
- ❖ **Deliver dances of salvation, healing and deliverance in our prisons**
- ❖ **On the beaches do a dance that brings relaxation but at the same time hope**
- ❖ **Go to those who are confined to their homes and deliver this 'fresh bread' to them**

The kingdom of heaven suffers violence at the hand of the enemy, so let us not forget what Jesus said in Luke 10:19: "Behold, I give unto you power to tread upon serpents and scorpions and over all the power of the enemy: and nothing shall hurt you." God is calling us to dance to a tune that will bring harmony in heaven as we move rhythmically with His army of angels and overpower ill-tuned instruments of hell with an increasingly strong dance of praise and worship. Jesus has already established the way for us in terms of worship. Why are we still hesitant when God has given us the right tools of application?

Remember, the enemy has blinded the eyes and deafened the ears of our people and we need to know that God desires all men to be saved. Look around you: the fields are ripe and ready for harvest, but where are the labourers?[15] I challenge you as one of those who have been called to propagate the kingdom, be like the twelve disciples who walked away from what they could achieve in the natural to secure an everlasting inheritance in Jesus Christ.

Let us build communities where Jesus can dwell, made not of violence but of praise in dance. Let us step together on the pulse beat because our purpose is to dance using our feet to trample demonic forces that bombard, influence and distract our children and youths. Allow every muscle to be like a finely tuned instrument as we allow the Holy Spirit to give us wings to soar like an eagle.

---

[15] Matthew 9:37

WHOSE AM I?

Jesus, in Mark 8:34b & 35 says, "Whosoever will come after Me, let him deny himself, and take up the cross and follow me. For whosoever will save his life shall lose it; but whosoever shall lose his life for my sake and the gospel's, the same shall save it."

Synonyms

Deny	=	forsake all
Take up	=	carry, lift
Follow	=	go or come after, accompany, keep to (path), conform to

The words mentioned above give a direct command to all those who love the Lord Jesus Christ. Once we become a part of the family of God, heavy demands are placed on us as dancers. Delivery of His word should therefore be practical and straightforward. Denying the things that pleased me more was hard but the Holy Spirit guided me along the winding road to a river with cool and refreshing water for that final immersion. As I dipped in the warm and soothing waters my feet, hands and entire body began to move to a rhythm that speaks of transformation in the arts.

Fresh bread for the diligent seekers is available for those who dance the Lord's dance. This rhythm brings a new dimension to worship where the dancer comes prepared by the Holy Spirit to spontaneously move through the aisle, tearing and cutting down all heaviness, lukewarmness, complacency and disharmony in the worship service.

This is a dance of completeness, penetrating the heart, making ready the bride for the coming of our Lord Jesus Christ, and the consummation of the marriage feast.[16]

HERE IS THE TABLE SPREAD FOR US

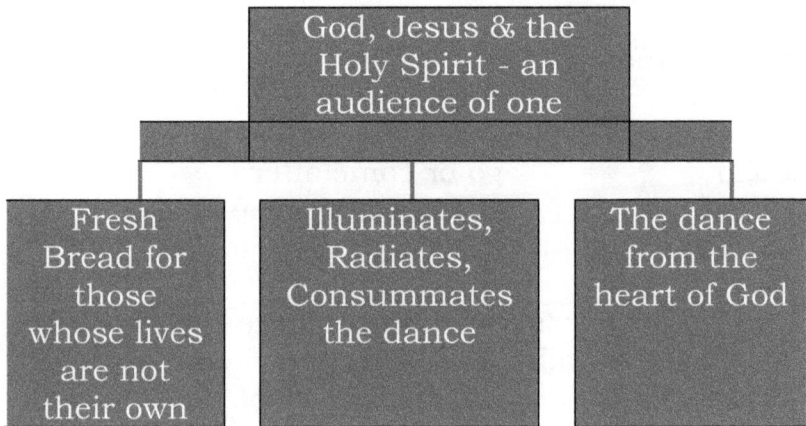

	God, Jesus & the Holy Spirit - an audience of one	
Fresh Bread for those whose lives are not their own	Illuminates, Radiates, Consummates the dance	The dance from the heart of God

---

[16] Revelation 9:19

WHO AM I?[17]
A scarred and broken vessel
He found and called it His
Filled with sin and scorn
That He only can reform

WHO AM I?
Purpose is just His goal
To accomplish for His church
What He had on His mind
Before the foundation of the earth

WHO AM I?
He stripped, reshaped and moulded
To make something worth looking at
That's whom he chose, He ordained
He anointed, sent and continued to protect

WHOSE AM I?
Enthralled and embedded is this life in Him
Going without questioning
Following where He leads me
To a river where the water is refreshing

WHOSE AM I?
The dance is His joy
Self-denial and obedience, nothing less
Required to take His cross and lose myself in Him
Running, touching, holding, never letting go
In His presence I must stay
For the sake of the gospel of Christ

Question
Whose Are You? Whose dance do you dance?

---

[17] Written by C Patrica Noble

PRAY THIS PRAYER WITH ME

Lord I rededicate this temple to you. Use it for your Glory. The negative things I give to you. Where I am weak, give me your strength. Where I lack confidence, give me a spirit of boldness. Let this dance be not about my abilities and accomplishments, but a dance that speaks and moves through your spirit, one that speaks about you, one that speaks life and not death, one that evokes righteousness, peace, love and joy in the Holy Ghost. May you always be pleased in what I give to you. In the name Of Jesus Christ, Amen.

CONCLUSION

Isaiah 61:1-3
"The Spirit of the Lord God is upon Me,
Because the LORD has anointed me to preach
good tidings to the poor;
He has sent Me to heal the brokenhearted,
To proclaim liberty to the captives,
And the opening of the prison to those who are
bound;
To proclaim the acceptable year of the Lord,
And the day of vengeance of our God;
To comfort all who mourn,
To console those who mourn in Zion,
To give them beauty for ashes,
The oil of joy for mourning,
The garment of praise for the spirit of heaviness;
That they may be called trees of righteousness,
The planting of the Lord, that He may be
glorified."

This passage depicts the essence of the new dance that God desires for His people. It is an affirmation of the abundant life that God wants us to come into as this new dance is delivered on the highways and byways. That God anointed Jesus was obvious throughout His entire ministry; He didn't have to tell anyone about His baptism with the resting of the dove on Him for them to believe Him. He walked in the anointing of the Holy Spirit, therefore victory was evident in every situation.

The dancer/worshipper should walk in this anointing. The busy streets are strung with hurting people yearning for compassion, searching for an identity; where are the dancers to demonstrate movements of hope? People are longing for rhythmic, radical dance which speaks to their situation and says there is hope. Creation is waiting and groaning for this visible form of radical worship which will set the captives free.

Let us all go down to the threshing floor where God can do His sifting work in us as He brings His wonderful redemptive plan to completion.

May the dance you do reflect Jesus Christ, the Anointed One.

ABOUT THE AUTHOR

Cynthia Patrica Noble was called into full-time Christian dance ministry in 1996, having previously taught academic subjects and dance for twenty years in various primary and secondary schools in Jamaica, West Indies. She was subsequently ordained as a minister of dance in 2005, and served at the Portmore Lane Covenant Community Church as the head of the dance ministry.

She is a trained teacher and a graduate of Shortwood Teacher's College and holds a Diploma in Dance in Education from The Edna Manley School of the Visual and Performing Arts. Cynthia, or 'Auntie Pat' as she is affectionately called, is also the founder of Praise Academy of Dance, Jamaica, Barbados and Trinidad and presently holds the position of Artistic Director of Praise Academy of Dance, Jamaica.

In October 2014 Cynthia received the Badge of Honour for Meritorious service for contribution to culture in the area of Dance and Culture from the Governor General of Jamaica, Sir Patrick Allen.

She also received the Flame Award from the International Christian Dance Fellowship Foundation, based in Australia, in July 2012 for her outstanding service to Christian dance ministry on an international level.

In October 2011, she received the Bronze Musgrave Medal for recognition of her contribution to the field of dance from the Institute of Jamaica.

Cynthia's passion is to see the redemption of the dance and its restoration in every heart, home, church, community and the nations at large. The essence of the new dance will cause the heartbeat of God to be in tune with our heartbeat, so that unity in spreading the gospel through dance will be automatic.

Contact Information:

Tel: (876) 883-2795)
Email: patricanoble@yahoo.com
Website:
http://praiseacademyofdancejamaica.com

www.ingramcontent.com/pod-product-compliance
Lightning Source LLC
Chambersburg PA
CBHW052140090426
42741CB00009B/2158